CATS SET IV

HIMALAYAN CATS

Nancy Furstinger
ABDO Publishing Company

visit us at
www.abdopub.com

Published by ABDO Publishing Company, 4940 Viking Drive, Edina, Minnesota 55435.
Copyright © 2006 by Abdo Consulting Group, Inc. International copyrights reserved in
all countries. No part of this book may be reproduced in any form without written
permission from the publisher. The Checkerboard Library™ is a trademark and logo of
ABDO Publishing Company.

Printed in the United States.

Cover Photo: Ron Kimball
Interior Photos: Animals Animals pp. 9, 19, 20; Corbis pp. 5, 7, 21; PhotoEdit p. 17;
    Ron Kimball pp. 11, 12, 13, 15

Series Coordinator: Megan Murphy
Editors: Stephanie Hedlund, Megan Murphy
Art Direction: Neil Klinepier

Library of Congress Cataloging-in-Publication Data

Furstinger, Nancy.
    Himalayan cats / Nancy Furstinger.
        p. cm. -- (Cats. Set IV)
    Includes bibliographical references and index.
    ISBN 1-59679-266-3
        1. Himalayan cat--Juvenile literature. I. Title.

SF449.H55F87 2005
636.8'3--dc22

                                                          2005040352

CONTENTS

Lions, Tigers, and Cats

Ancient Egyptians believed the cat was sacred. More than 4,000 years ago, they worshipped the cat in temples. They believed the cat symbolized prosperity. Sometimes, these pets were mummified and placed in special tombs after death.

Descendants of these sacred cats continue to be prized around the world. Today, more than 40 **breeds** of **domestic** cats exist. These cats are members of the **Felidae** family, which contains 38 different species.

Wildcats are also in the Felidae family. These big cats include lions, tigers, jaguars, and leopards. Big and small cats grasp and tear their prey with claws and teeth. However, big cats cannot purr and small cats cannot roar.

You don't have to travel far to see the wild relatives of domestic cats. They are often found at the zoo. And like their smaller cousins, big cats don't like baths either!

HIMALAYAN CATS

The Himalayan cat **breed** began as an experiment in **genetics**. In the 1930s, scientists bred Siamese and Persian cats together. They wanted to see if the Siamese's color pattern could be passed to the long-haired Persian.

From this experiment, the first **pointed** longhair cat was born. This cat was recognized as the beginning of the Himalayan breed. Throughout the 1950s, other breeding programs worked to establish a Persian-type breed with Siamese markings.

These programs officially introduced the Himalayan into the **Felidae** family. The **Cat Fanciers' Association** recognized Himalayans as a breed in 1957. Today, these cats are considered a subclass of the Persian.

The Himalayan cat was named after the Himalayas, a mountain range in Asia. This name was chosen because there are goats and rabbits with similar color patterns that live in this region.

QUALITIES

Himalayans combine the best **traits** from the Persian and the Siamese. Like their Persian cousins, they are sweet tempered and calm. Like Siamese, they are outgoing and playful.

Himalayans adore attention. They prefer to be in the center of things. They are happiest when being admired and showing off. Daily cuddling and combing sessions keep them purring.

These cats make perfect indoor pets. They don't like jumping or climbing and are not very adventurous. They like to follow their family around and snuggle in laps.

Himalayans might engage you in lively games. Since they love people, one of their favorite games is follow-the-leader! They also welcome new toys to toss around and chase.

Himalayans have a quiet meow that they rarely use. Their voice is slightly louder than a full Persian, but softer than a Siamese.

COAT AND COLOR

The Himalayan has the long, thick coat of a Persian. But, it has the distinct color pattern of a Siamese. The Himalayan carries the **pointing** gene that causes this coloration.

The pointing gene uses body temperature to determine color. The ears, face, tail, and legs are usually colder than the rest of the body. So, the fur in these areas is darker. But in warmer areas, the gene prevents the darker color from developing.

There are about 20 colors of Himalayans to choose from. One popular color is the seal point. This is the typical Siamese color. There are also tortoiseshell and **tabby** patterns. Most Himalayans have bright blue eyes. Some have gold eyes.

This Himalayan exhibits the flame point, or red point, color pattern. This pattern features red or orange point markings.

SIZE

The Himalayan is a medium to large cat. Its body shape is square, yet rounded.

Short, strong legs support the Himalayan's stout frame. Both the shoulders and rump are equally massive. A short, bushy tail tapers to a slightly rounded tip.

Himalayans have also been called the colorpoint longhair, colorpoint Persian, or pointed Persian.

These cats have large, round heads with full cheeks. Tiny ears are positioned low on the Himalayan's head. The short, snub nose sits between large, round eyes.

While Himalayans are bigger cats in general, males typically weigh more than females.

CARE

Cats spend much of the day licking their fur. They use their rough tongues to groom themselves. However, long-haired cats also need human help to prevent tangles and hair balls.

Start grooming your Himalayan when it is a kitten. Groom it each day using a wide-toothed comb or a wire brush. During spring and early summer, Himalayans shed quite a bit. Extra grooming at this time keeps mats from forming.

A bath every three months will also keep the Himalayan's coat dazzling. Use a shampoo made specifically for cats. Some Himalayans get tearstains around their eyes. A moistened cotton ball will remove these brown stains.

Along with grooming, your cat needs a yearly checkup and **vaccines** at the veterinarian's office. While there, the veterinarian can also **neuter** or **spay** your pet.

Cats have a natural instinct to bury their waste. So, be sure to provide a litter box for your pet to use. And, don't forget to clean it daily!

FEEDING

Feed your Himalayan the same food it ate in its first home. Later, you can slowly blend in another brand. If you've adopted a picky eater, try several different foods to see what your cat likes best.

Cats are meat eaters by nature. So, they need a variety of proteins in their diet. Commercial cat foods will provide your cat with the **nutrients** it needs. Most brands contain proteins such as chicken and fish.

There are three different kinds of commercial cat food. They are canned, semimoist, and dry. Follow the feeding instructions on the food label. It will tell you how much to feed your Himalayan based on its age, weight, and health.

Cats cannot grind or crush their food. They must cut it with their sharp teeth instead.

Cats enjoy having a set pattern. They look forward to being served their supper at a specific time. Remember to always have fresh water available, too. Some cats enjoy milk, but others experience stomach problems from it.

KITTENS

Female Himalayan cats are **pregnant** for about 63 to 65 days. The mother gives birth to approximately four kittens in each **litter**.

Kittens are born completely white with pink noses. Faint **point** markings start filling in during the first week. The pattern might take up to 18 months to develop.

At birth, kittens are blind and deaf. For the first three weeks, they only drink their mother's milk. After that, they can start eating solid food. They also begin to play and explore.

Himalayan kittens should be gently cuddled. This will create calm, friendly pets. Early handling will also prepare them for daily grooming. When kittens are 9 to 12 weeks old, they can go home with new families.

All kittens are born with blue eyes. But as they get older, their eye color may change.

BUYING A KITTEN

A Himalayan can live between 15 and 20 years. It will become very attached to its family. If you are considering this **breed**, make sure someone can groom it every day.

The Himalayan has grown rapidly in popularity. Today, it is one of the top breeds. Breeders sell **purebred** kittens and retired show cats. Himalayan kittens and cats can be adopted from animal shelters, too.

Kitten or cat, the creature you choose should be healthy, curious, and friendly. Check

This talented Himalayan wants you to pay attention to it!

The lilac points on these Himalayan kittens are already starting to fill in.

to make sure that the fur is glossy and the eyes are clear. These are signs your Himalayan will be a healthy pet for years to come.

GLOSSARY

breed - a group of animals sharing the same appearance and characteristics. A breeder is a person who raises animals. Raising animals is often called breeding them.

Cat Fanciers' Association (CFA) - a group that sets the standards for judging all breeds of cats.

domestic - animals that are tame.

Felidae - the scientific Latin name for the cat family.

genetics - a branch of biology that deals with heredity.

litter - all of the kittens born at one time to a mother cat.

neuter (NOO-tuhr) - to remove a male animal's reproductive organs.

nutrient - a substance found in food and used in the body to promote growth, maintenance, and repair.

points - the darkened areas of certain coat patterns. This pattern is also called colorpoint or pointed.

pregnant - having one or more babies growing within the body.

purebred - an animal whose parents are both from the same breed.

spay - to remove a female animal's reproductive organs.

tabby - the striped or splotchy pattern of a cat's coat. A cat with this pattern is often called a tabby cat.

trait - a quality that distinguishes one person or group from another.

vaccine (vak-SEEN) - a shot given to animals or humans to prevent them from getting an illness or disease.

WEB SITES

To learn more about Himalayan cats, visit ABDO Publishing Company on the World Wide Web at **www.abdopub.com**. Web sites about these cats are featured on our Book Links page. These links are routinely monitored and updated to provide the most current information available.

INDEX